I0786271

Copyright 2018

Jerry Wyant

Cult 45

Can America Survive Trumpism?

By Jerry Wyant

Table of Contents

****

Take a minute to let this sink in. We are under attack. At no time in America's history would this happen without the entire country unifying around a strong and appropriate response.

Until now.

Page 42

****

****

Instead of seriously investigating the attack on America, Republicans in Congress investigate and threaten our own intelligence services.

Page 44

****

****

Trump is telling his followers to believe Putin rather than all our own intelligence professionals.

Let that one sink in.

Page 45

****

****

All institutions within the constitutional system of checks and balances have come under attack by Trumpism.

Page 47

****

****

Since his cult is also the base of the party, Republican congresspersons who don't show loyalty to Trump lose the support of their own voters.

This effectively neuters Article I powers and subjugates the legislature to the executive.

Page 47

****

****

Trump has appointed cabinet secretaries who have no experience or expertise in their own departments. Their only qualification seems to be complete loyalty and subversion to Trump himself.

Page 48

****

****

Trump and his cult are working to create a dictatorship in America to replace our constitutional republic. I never thought this could ever happen in the United States. But I'm sure Putin is proud.

Page 51

****

****

Trump lies, and lies, and lies.

He's not the first politician to tell a lie, of course.

But he has taken the art of lying to a much higher level.

Page 54

****

****

There are reasons Trump and his allies could be desperately trying to undermine the investigation by attacking the credibility of the investigators.

Innocence is not one of those reasons.

Page 56

****

****

They don't need facts because they know what they see.

Page 60

****

****

Of course, these people wouldn't see themselves as being part of the problem. They are the "true" Americans that this nation was founded for.

The problem is those "others".

Page 60

****

****

It's easier to treat people as "others" if you think of them as somewhat less than human.

That philosophy has held up very well for "real Americans" for a long time, even as the definition of who the "others" are has changed.

Page 61

****

****

Even law-abiding Americans of Hispanic descent are suspect; they're "illegal" unless they can prove otherwise.

Page 63

****

****

Undocumented Hispanics are not terrorists, and they are not a threat to national security.

Page 64

****

****

Whatever the problem is, real or perceived, these "real Americans" have a scapegoat to blame it on. "We" aren't the problem, the "others" are the problem.

Page 64

****

****

"Others" are taking over the neighborhood; a neighborhood created by "real Americans".

There is a feeling among "real Americans" that they simply must "take their country back".

It starts with fear, but it soon turns to hatred.

Page 66

****

****

Many "real Americans" begin to think of the "others" as having somewhat less than full human status.

If they aren't full humans, then the "real Americans" won't feel guilty about denying them basic human dignity.

Page 67

****

22

****

Dehumanizing "others" allows "real Americans" to justify an extremist, hard line agenda for dealing with real and perceived problems in society.

Page 67

****

****

Simplistic identification of problems.

Simplistic solutions.

Hatred of "others", who are less human.

Support law enforcement officers to the extent that they are tough on the "others".

Don't trust the government.

This is the formula used by self-proclaimed "real Americans"

Page 68

****

****

The "real Americans" who detest and dehumanize the "others" and distrust the government may have begun as small groups of locals, but together they constitute a large media market.

New national media was created to take advantage of this market.

Page 69

****

****

Need proof?

Go to the timeline.

Page 72

****

****

Trump has a firm grip on the bigot vote. It is his base of support.

Republicans in Congress are afraid to speak out against Trump's many (and I should add, daily) attacks on basic human decency. They feel they can't afford to have his base voters turn against them.

Alas, his base is also their base.

Page 72

****

****

For now, the Republican Party is Trump's party.

Page 73

****

****

Trump plays the part of cult leader very well.

Page 73

****

****

He is at his best when he holds public rallies for his supporters.

These supporters cheer loudest for the most hateful rhetoric.

They boo everyone he calls an enemy.

Page 73

****

****

Everything is someone else's fault to the point where American institutions, America's promises, America's global standing, American sovereignty, and democracy itself do not matter.

They don't matter to him, and they don't matter to his followers.

And this is where the danger of this cultism really lies.

Page 74

****

****

Trump does not adhere to historic Republican principles.

His supporters, most of whom have espoused these same principles throughout their lives, forfeit their own principles in favor of being loyal to Trump.

Page 77

****

****

Professional analysts have determined that Trump speaks on a 4th grade level.

Page 80

****

****

If they support Trump because of the economy, they just might take away that support when the economy turns sour.

Page 82

****

****

What kinds of people support Trump?

Page 84

****

****

Our national right to self-determination is at stake. The American way of life is at stake. The United States Constitution is at stake. Democracy itself is at stake.

Why would Trump supporters be willing to risk all of this and continue to support him? What could be more important to them?

Page 88

****

****

Trump supporters have access to the same information that scares the rest of us to death.

Page 88

****

****

Willful ignorance is not a virtue when so much is on the line.

Willful ignorance, in fact, is a character flaw.

Page 89

****

****

You don't have to be a Trump supporter to have character flaws.

But you do have to have character flaws to be a Trump supporter.

It is a necessary condition.

Page 91

****

****

We can stop Trump.

The question is whether we can stop Trumpism.

Page 96

****

****

These are not normal times.

Page 99

****

The Worst Crisis in America Since the Civil War

The United States is under attack. We have been attacked by a hostile foreign power. Our national sovereignty is at stake because of this attack. Democracy itself is at stake because of this attack.

Take a minute to let that sink in. We are under attack. At no time in America's history would this happen without the entire country unifying around a strong and appropriate response. We could always be sure that we would repel the attack and punish the attackers in such a way that no one would ever dare to launch a similar attack again.

Until now.

Think about it. While our national sovereignty is under attack, we are not responding as if it is as much of a threat as it really is. Why are we not taking proper steps to stop this attack?

The answer is plain and simple: Trumpism. The cult of Trumpism.

***

We have institutions set up to prevent this situation from ever occurring. First and foremost, we have the U.S. Constitution. The Constitution includes checks and balances which the founders thought would be sufficient. But the founders didn't count on a cult taking control of these institutions, preventing them from performing their constitutional duties.

The cult of Trumpism has become the base of the Republican Party. The Republican Party is in control of all branches of the federal government and is also in control of many state governments. Sadly, most Republican members of Congress would rather forfeit their constitutional duties of oversight than face a backlash from the base of their own party. To them, personal reelection is more important than their sworn duties to defend and uphold the Constitution. They would rather risk the loss of America's right to self-determination; they would rather risk the end of democracy itself than face the prospect of being primaried by Trump and his cult of followers.

Let that one sink in. I said, "most Republican members of Congress". Some Republicans have chosen not to run for reelection. Most have caved in to Trumpism. This includes all of those in leadership positions.

Since their party is in control of Congress, Republicans hold all the key leadership positions, including committee chairs. Republicans decide which bills come to the floor for discussion and votes. Republicans decide what gets investigated and what does not get investigated. Yet their decisions are tainted by their abdication of duty. Republican leadership states publicly that they won't allow a bill to be voted on unless they have assurance that the president supports it.

Republican committee chairpersons put on a sham of an investigation into Russian interference in our election system. Instead of seriously investigating the attack on America, they investigate and threaten our own intelligence services. Instead of checking out obvious leads into the attack on our nation, they say something to the effect of, "nothing to see here", and then attack the intelligence professionals who continue to follow leads and search for the truth.

This danger to our sovereignty is brought to you by the cult of Trumpism.

Trump claims to have had no part in the Russian attack on America. I trust that the Special Counsel investigation will provide the answer to whether Trump's claim on this subject is true or not.

We do know that Russia attacked America; we know that Trump initially denied that Russia had attacked our election; we know that when evidence of this attack became clear, Trump changed his story to be that no one in his campaign had any contacts with Russians during the time frame in question; we know that Trump refused to punish Russia for such an attack; we know that when proof of many contacts between Trump campaign staff and Russia was made public, Trump personally falsified stories about such contacts; we know that Trump has attempted to distance himself from those campaign staffers implicated; we know that Trump's story now is that he personally – regardless of what his staff was doing – had nothing to do with Russia during the election.

In fine circular argument fashion, Trump goes back to his original story. He had nothing to do with Russia's attack on America because such an attack never took place. Trump's source? Vladimir Putin. Putin told him that there was no attack, so Trump is telling his followers to believe Putin rather than all our own intelligence professionals.

Let that one sink in.

According to the cult of Trumpism, no "collusion" took place between Trump and Russia. It's clear to the rest of us, based on evidence which is publicly known, that some collusion did in fact take place. We know that the investigation has already netted several indictments and guilty pleas.

Which specific laws were broken, and who else broke those laws besides the ones already charged or settled, is yet to be determined.

Perhaps the Special Counsel will not find anything to charge Trump with. The only way to know for sure is to let the investigation play out. But Trump's changing stories indicate that he is hiding something. Trump's constant attack on the investigators and the press indicate that he is hiding something.

Despite public denials to the contrary, Trump and some in his cult have openly obstructed the investigation. This also indicates that he is hiding something. Plus, obstruction of justice by itself is a crime and an impeachable offense.

***

The Constitution was designed as a system of checks and balances precisely to prevent what is happening in America today. This system is the foundation of the American form of government.

All institutions within the constitutional system of checks and balances have come under attack by Trumpism.

***

Legislative branch (Article I of the Constitution)

Trump's own party is in control of the legislature. But any member who doesn't echo Trump's world view is attacked by Trump and his cult. Any member who doesn't show obedience to Trump is attacked by Trump and his cult.

Since his cult is also the base of the party, Republican congresspersons who don't show loyalty to Trump lose the support of their own voters. This effectively neuters Article I powers and subjugates the legislature to the executive.

***

Executive branch (Article II of the Constitution)

Trump has appointed cabinet secretaries who have no experience or expertise in their own departments. Their only qualification seems to be complete loyalty and subversion to Trump himself.

In some cases, he has appointed people whose political philosophy is in direct opposition to the work of their departments. For example, we have a Secretary of Education who doesn't believe in public education. We have a Secretary of Labor who doesn't believe in supporting worker rights.

Trump also demands that the nation's intelligence community, part of the executive branch, work to protect him personally rather than work for the people of the United States. When they perform the duties that they are sworn to do, rather than cave in to Trump's demands, he attacks them.

He fired James Comey. He has threatened the Attorney General, the Assistant Attorney General, and the Special Counsel with firing. Perhaps most ominous of all, he repeatedly attacks them verbally in public – to the point where his followers say they don't trust our intelligence professionals to investigate fairly.

This is a very dangerous consequence of Trumpism. What is the cult going to do when the results of the investigation are made public, and the results prove misconduct by Trump and his associates? He will say, "I told you the investigation was an unfair political attack on me. I told you I am innocent."

He has his followers conditioned for this. What will be their response? Will riots break out? Will America's institutions survive?

***

Judicial branch (Article III of the Constitution)

Trump's shady personal life has placed him in a position to have been involved in many legal actions. While cases are pending, he puts public pressure on judges to rule in his favor. When judges rule against him, he publicly berates them. He even called out one judge because of the judge's Mexican heritage.

Trump's tendency to berate judges who rule against him has continued for cases involving his official actions as president.

Also, Trump wants to bypass the legal system altogether so that he can implement his inhumane immigration policy with no due process and with no oversight.

Trump and his supporters love to chant, "lock her up!", a reference to Hillary Clinton, who has been thoroughly investigated over many trumped-up (no pun intended) right-wing media claims. All these investigations, including those being led by anti-Clinton Republicans, resulted in no crimes being found. Yet they still shout, "lock her up!".

Not only does this promote a denial of judicial due process, it promotes a tactic used only in a Banana Republic: jail your political opponents. The cult of Trumpism is complicit in this despicable display.

***

The First Amendment to the Constitution

It's difficult to list all the times Trump has attacked the First Amendment. His repeated use of the term "fake news" and his derogatory nicknames for news organizations is a direct attack on the First Amendment. Not only that, but he is attacking a free and independent press, which is an essential institution for a free populace and for democracy itself.

His Muslim travel ban is an attack on the First Amendment. His verbal attacks on protestors – football players protesting racial injustice and teenage survivors of mass shootings, just to name a couple of examples – are attacks on the First Amendment.

***

All these attacks on the Constitution and American institutions with constitutional authority add up to one thing: Trump and his cult are working to create a dictatorship in America to replace our constitutional republic. I never thought this could ever happen in the United States. But I'm sure Putin is proud.

In addition to the constitutional issues mentioned above, Trump has done tremendous damage to the presidency itself. This should surprise no one who has been paying attention all along. Trump supporters knew what kind of person they were voting for in 2016.

He has a documented history of racism and promoting conspiracy theories. He became the face of the birther movement. To help himself get elected, he called Mexicans "rapists" and accused Ted Cruz's father of conspiring to kill President Kennedy.

As president, he called white supremacy advocates "good people". As president, he said that families fleeing violence in Central America were "infesting" the United States. As president, he has broken American law by not allowing asylum seekers to seek asylum. He has taken children away from families fleeing violence. He has given the parents a choice: denounce your claim of asylum, accept deportation back to the dangerous country you are fleeing from, OR YOU WILL NEVER SEE YOUR CHILDREN AGAIN. Yes, kidnapping children from desperate parents, and holding them for ransom.

As president, he has repeatedly attacked the intelligence of black congresspersons.

Trump has a documented history of mistreatment of women. He cheated on each of his wives. He has had several credible claims of sexual misconduct leveled against him. He admitted to sexual assault on the infamous Access Hollywood tape. When women publicly disagree with him, he attacks their physical appearances.

Trump supporters knew all this before they voted for him. They know that he doesn't respect women. Trump supporters must know that someday their own children and grandchildren will hold them accountable for supporting such an immoral person to be the face of America to the world and a role model for our youth. Yet their support doesn't waver.

Trump's life as a real estate wheeler-dealer includes shady deals with many shady characters around the world. Although this is all still under investigation, enough facts are known publicly to raise red flags about illegal activities such as money laundering, and perhaps quid pro quo regarding presidential favors to America's enemies.

He hired a shady character to be his campaign manager. He hired another shady character to be his personal attorney. He had other shady characters working on his campaign. Stay tuned; some of these shady characters are now cooperating with the Special Counsel, who undoubtedly has much more evidence at his disposal.

Trump lies, and lies, and lies. He's not the first politician to tell a lie, of course. But he has taken the art of lying to a much higher level. He lies about big things. He lies about little things. When he is caught in a lie, he doubles down with more lies. When all else fails, he blames his lies on someone else: President Obama, or his favorite, "Crooked Hillary".

When Trump says, "believe me", most of us have learned not to believe him. But his followers still do, demonstrating the power of the cult of Trumpism.

Trump has destroyed our relationships with long-standing military and economic allies. He has set out to destroy our international alliances and renege on America's promises to the world. He has publicly insulted many leaders of democratic nations, yet he only has good words to say about the idea of a powerful dictatorship, and especially about Vladimir Putin.

Trump left the G7 Summit, which he deliberately undermined by insulting our important trading partners from democratic nations, then went straight to a meeting with the dictator of North Korea – where he praised the dictator for his ability to keep his people under his power.

Our traditional allies no longer trust the United States. They can no longer be assured that we will keep our word. Trump refused to acknowledge that the United States under his presidency would honor the common defense pact of NATO until public pressure forced him to belatedly announce that he accepts Article 5. He kept the entire world on edge before doing so. And when he did, his words were less than 100% convincing, given his propensity to say one thing and do another.

Can NATO members really trust us? Can we trust them to come to our aid, when our president continues to insult them?

Under Trump, we renege on treaties and other important international agreements. Our world is less safe. Multilateral agreements no longer include the United States. Agreements in which we took the lead in arranging are now going on without us, as the United States becomes more isolated under Trump's "America First" strategy.

Security agreements, military agreements, and trade agreements have been wiped out by one man. The world is less safe because of Trump; America's defense is less safe because of Trump; American businesses are losing out on important markets because of Trump.

Trump has unilaterally created a trade war which is unsustainable. The trade war has just begun as of this writing, but soon every American will feel it's economic pain. How low will the economy sink before Trump's followers recognize that his policies are to blame? Meanwhile, with his trade war, Trump could not resist taking pot shots at our most important economic and defense partners. The trade war is a national security issue. Trump has verbally attacked and threatened at least one American business for reacting to his trade war in its own self-interest.

He takes pot shots at our most important allies, but not at Putin and Russia. Trump secretly invited Russian diplomats into the Oval Office and revealed top secret information to them. The only reason we know about this is because pictures were published on Russian state media. He kept this meeting secret from American intelligence and American media, but not from Russian intelligence and Russian media.

Even before his inauguration, Trump's transition team illegally met with Russians and promised to undo sanctions imposed on Russia by the Obama administration. Stay tuned. The Special Counsel team has all the facts.

There are reasons Trump and his allies could be desperately trying to undermine the investigation by attacking the credibility of the investigators. Innocence is not one of those reasons.

How Did We Get Here?

If we want to trace the events which led up to our current situation, we need to go way back in time. The stage was set long before Trump. Perhaps it has been this way for centuries. The stage was set long ago, but there were a few missing pieces.

The missing pieces which led to Trump and the current crisis were only added recently. The missing pieces were a national media presence whose sole purpose was to exploit willing participants, technology advances which include social media, and hostile foreign powers willing and able to use technology to interfere in America's sovereignty.

Let's start with the pieces which have been in place for a long time. Picture this scenario:

A few locals are sitting in a tavern. The topic of conversation turns to "what is wrong with this country?" Everybody thinks he knows the answer. These people aren't experts. They are just everyday Joes. They consider themselves to be "real Americans", distinguishing themselves from those "others" who are the source of everything wrong with America.

This scenario is playing out in virtually every corner of America. They might not be experts, but everybody has a strong opinion. They are sure they have the solutions, and their solutions are indeed simple ones.

Their opinions are based on emotion. The natural tendency in this situation is for participants to take a hardline stance. They have no need to study the issues involved. They have no need to consider the consequences of their solutions. Those are the kinds of things the despised egg-headed liberals think about. Liberals are always getting in the way of simple solutions.

"Real Americans" have "real" solutions which are simple and obvious. "Real Americans" don't need to be reminded of the principles on which America was founded or of constitutional restrictions. If the Constitution gets in the way of their solutions, then the Constitution is wrong. The same is true of facts. They don't need facts because they know what they see.

Of course, these people wouldn't see themselves as being part of the problem. They are the "true" Americans that this nation was founded for. The problem is those "others". The solution is to get tough on the "others".

Leave the "regular" law-abiding Americans alone and quit catering to the "others". That is the solution.

Just who are the "others"? Once upon a time, the "others" were called "savages", known today as Native Americans. They stood in the way of what white men wanted to do, so they had to be systematically removed. After all, "savages" are a lower life form than "real" humans. It's easier to treat people as "others" if you think of them as somewhat less than human. That philosophy has held up very well for "real Americans" for a long time, even as the definition of who the "others" are has changed.

The "others" also included slaves. Slaves weren't considered as human but rather as property. They were a necessary evil. They had to be kept in their place. Not only were they property, but they were different. Their skin was black. "Real Americans" concluded that it was the black skin which made them inferior to white men. Even free blacks had to be somewhat less than human.

More than 150 years after the abolition of slavery, black Americans are still the "others", which makes it easy for many of these "real Americans" to think of them as subhuman.

The "others" have always included immigrants, but only certain immigrants. The "real Americans" were not native Americans, who were "others". "Real Americans" were of immigrant stock. The immigrants who were "others" were different kinds of immigrants. They came here to steal our jobs. They came here to change our culture. They spoke different languages, or at least a different type of English than "real" Americans. Some of them had a different religion than "real Americans".

The immigrants who were "others" seemed to keep to themselves. They were different, and they weren't fitting into the "real" American culture. Wave after wave of white European immigrants fit this pattern.

But a funny thing happened with each new wave of such immigrants. Eventually, they did fit in. It might have taken a generation to fully integrate into the "real" American society, but they became "real Americans". They acquired the speech and language of their new home. Their religions were accepted, or at least tolerated.

And just like "real Americans", they joined in the chorus denouncing new waves of immigrants who followed them; immigrants who were different from them. "Others", if they had white skin, became "real Americans", who took to denouncing "others". This is a sad truth from American history.

Hispanics make up the current wave of immigrants. Many of them are fleeing for their lives. Many are seeking asylum, and the United States Government shows little concern for their plight. They have faced the same kinds of backlashes as previous waves of immigrants: backlashes against culture, language, religion. But they have an additional barrier: their skin color. They are being labeled as hardened criminals. They are being blamed for crime, terrorism, and the drug trade. They are considered a threat to national security.

The backlash against Hispanics is often labeled as support for law and order. If any Hispanic commits a crime, then both legal and illegal immigration of Hispanics must be stopped.

It's all Mexico's fault, and we need a wall to protect our southern border.

Even law-abiding Americans of Hispanic descent are suspect; they're "illegal" unless they can prove otherwise.

According to "real Americans", Hispanics are criminals by the very fact that they broke our laws coming across the border. Thus, we must preserve law and order.

The same isn't said of the many European immigrants who have broken the law by overstaying their visas. Hispanics are treated much differently.

They are considered dangerous. Yet, the crime rate among undocumented Hispanics in America is lower than the overall crime rate among Americans. Undocumented Hispanics are not terrorists, and they are not a threat to national security.

The "others" also include LGBTQ individuals, peaceful protestors of institutionalized injustice, victims of gun violence who have the audacity to speak out, and women – including victims of sexual abuse.

Whatever the problem is, real or perceived, these "real Americans" have a scapegoat to blame it on. "We" aren't the problem, the "others" are the problem.

***

Is crime a problem? Rough up the criminals, or at least let the police rough them up. Criminals deserve it, regardless of what the Constitution says. Then, if the criminals survive the brutality, lock them up and throw away the key. Just remember that crime is defined as those offenses which those "others" tend to commit. Any violation of human rights by "real Americans" in retaliation for crimes committed by "others" is not a crime. After all, real Americans must "take their country back".

Is welfare a problem? It certainly is, according to these "real Americans". After all, they know what they see. They see themselves and other "real Americans" working hard and paying taxes. Then they wait in line at the grocery store while the "others" in line ahead of them are getting free stuff from welfare. This gives "real Americans" the right to pass judgment on the choices made by "others". After all, "real Americans" have to pay taxes so that "others" can afford freebies.

These "others" should be out working for a living, but obviously they are lazy and prefer to live off the toil of "real Americans". The "others" are freeloaders, filling up the welfare rolls. Many of the "others" are Hispanic, so they are obviously here illegally. Therefore, the problem is "illegals" coming here to collect welfare and mooch off hard-working Americans. And they are doing it with the blessing of the government! Never mind checking to see if the facts match these conclusions: "Real Americans" know what they see. These "others" must be deported, and "real Americans" must oppose a government which caters to "others".

Is unemployment a problem? Obviously, these "others" are "illegals" who are stealing jobs from "real

Americans". We need to deport them so that we can get our jobs back. We know who they are by their brown skin and the fact that many of them aren't fluid in English.

That's another thing – "real Americans" have determined that we must pass a law requiring everybody to speak English. We certainly don't understand their language. For all we know, they might be plotting against us.

Never mind the fact that statistics show that these "others" create jobs. We "real Americans" know what we see.

And it goes on. Whatever the problem, these "real Americans" always have a scapegoat to blame. It's always the fault of "others".

These "real Americans" fear the "others". Maybe it's because their speech is different. Maybe it's because their culture is different. Maybe it's because their skin color is different. Maybe it's because their religion is different. Maybe they just act differently. Maybe "real Americans" fear that "others" are trying to change the culture away from the familiar.

"Others" are taking over the neighborhood; a neighborhood created by "real Americans". There is a feeling among "real Americans" that they simply must "take their country back". It starts with fear, but it soon turns to hatred.

Even worse, many "real Americans" begin to think of the "others" as having somewhat less than full human status. If they aren't full humans, then the "real Americans" won't feel guilty about denying them basic human dignity.

Dehumanizing "others" allows "real Americans" to justify an extremist, hard line agenda for dealing with real and perceived problems in society.

Who can these "real Americans" trust, other than each other? They certainly can't trust the government. The government creates problems. The government can't solve problems. What can "real Americans" do? They can sit around and complain about the government interfering in their lives. On election day, they can vote to "throw those bums out". But the situation never changes. They need to throw the new bums out next election cycle. What these "real Americans" do best is dehumanize the "others".

***

These types of conversations have been going on for centuries in America. Yes, the conversations take place in taverns, but it isn't just the beer speaking. Such conversations also take place in coffee shops, workplaces, churches, schools, family gatherings, or just about anywhere "real Americans" congregate.

By ignoring facts and letting emotions rule their thinking process, "real Americans" are perpetuating myths and conspiracy theories.

Simplistic identification of problems. Simplistic solutions. Hatred of "others", who are less human. Support law enforcement officers to the extent that they are tough on the "others". Don't trust the government. This is the formula used by local "real Americans" who have engaged in such conversations for all these years.

Versions of this scenario have been playing out across America since the very beginning.

***

No, it didn't start with Trump. It has been going on for centuries in communities across America. But something changed in more recent times which created a direct line from these conversations to Trumpism.

The "real Americans" who detest and dehumanize the "others" and distrust the government may have begun as small groups of locals, but together they constitute a large media market. New national media was created to take advantage of this market. Fox News and others have specifically targeted these "real Americans" as their customers. Now, "real Americans" have media to turn to; not as a source of truth, but to confirm their own biases.

"Real Americans" were targeted, and they willingly took the bait. Now they had "news" sources which were saying the same things they had been saying all along. The entire purpose of these types of media is to cater to the specific biases of this targeted audience.

National media taking advantage of these biases changed the landscape. It allowed these small groups to unite as a large bloc. Now, they could listen to someone who not only shared their biases but could give them universal talking points. As a large bloc, with common talking points, they suddenly had political power. Now, they could run for office while proudly and publicly proclaiming their biases.

We got a taste of this on a national level in 1994 when many of these "real Americans" were elected to the

House of Representatives. The Tea Party movement took this to a much higher level, beginning in 2010.

We ended up with many in Congress whose political views centered on "real Americans" vs "others". We ended up with people of shared biases forming the base of one of the two major political parties. We elected a government composed largely of people opposed to government. The resulting rise in political polarization was predictable.

Many "real Americans" whose focus was on demonizing "others" were already getting elected to Congress. It was only a matter of time before someone would come along and win the presidency by catering exclusively to the biases of these "real Americans".

These biases collectively have another name: bigotry. The "real Americans" referred to here are bigots who have become a large voting bloc in America.

***

This is where Donald Trump comes into the picture.

The story is still being written about how Trump managed to win the 2016 presidential election. How many votes were changed due to Russian and other Foreign attacks on social media? How many votes were changed because of email attacks and the subsequent

Wikileaks' carefully-timed and selective release of documents?

Besides social media and email attacks, what other foreign attacks on our system played a part in the outcome of the 2016 election? Did the Trump campaign's many contacts with Russians prove to be a difference maker in the election?

The FBI's public handling of the Hillary Clinton investigation, combined with utter silence on the fact that Trump was being investigated, certainly played a big role in the outcome. The timeline clearly shows this. What about Hillary being a "flawed candidate" who should have spent more time in specific battleground states? By the way, she did win the popular vote with a differential of nearly 3,000,000.

It's possible that any of the above made the difference between a Clinton presidency and a Trump presidency. We may never know the answers to all of these "what ifs". We will have much more information after the Mueller investigation is complete. But even if it can be determined that a difference was made, it is probably impossible to tell quantitatively exactly how many votes, and from which states, were affected.

But one thing is very clear: Hillary would have won in a landslide if not for the votes of bigots. Bigots formed

Trump's base of support, and he needed their votes to have a chance to win the election.

Need proof? Go to the timeline, starting with the beginning of the 2016 campaign and continuing through today. Every time Trump made an outrageously bigoted public comment, his poll numbers increased.

During the early days of the 2016 primary season, he soared from the back of the pack into what proved to be an insurmountably lead over the other 15 Republican candidates with his over-the-top rhetoric. Again, this is clear according to the timeline of events.

During his presidency, his poll numbers have increased with every bigoted comment and action taken against the "others". He further alienates those with valid concerns, but his popularity goes up with his base of support.

Obviously, this also means further political polarization.

Trump has a firm grip on the bigot vote. It is his base of support. Republicans in Congress are afraid to speak out against Trump's many (and I should add, daily) attacks on basic human decency. They feel they can't afford to have his base voters turn against them. Alas, his base is also their base.

This is reality in today's Republican Party. It won't change until Republicans finally realize that their future as a party depends on them seeking a different base of supporters. For now, the Republican Party is Trump's party.

Other Republicans are helpless to do anything about it, because Trump has a hold on the base of the Republican party the same way that a cult leader has a hold on his followers.

Trump plays the part of cult leader very well. He knows his followers are there because of his stances against the "others". He feeds off their bigotry by taking hateful rhetoric to new levels. He is at his best when he holds public rallies for his supporters. These supporters cheer loudest for the most hateful rhetoric. They boo everyone he calls an enemy.

Most importantly for a cult leader, Trump convinces his followers that he is the only one who can solve their problems.

He is the cult leader and his followers are his cult. They are the cult, and he is their messiah. They must take his side no matter what. This takes the "blame it on others" to a whole new level.

If he insults members of his own party, his followers take his side. When he changes his mind or changes his story, they take each of his sides. Every day when he tells lies big and small, they take his side. When he repeats conspiracy theories, they take his side. When he fights against everything that America has ever stood for, they take his side. When he insults our nation's allies and cozies up to brutal dictators, they take his side. When he attacks the First Amendment in both words and actions, they take his side.

When the whole world sees him breaking the law, they take his side as he shifts the blame from himself onto the American institutions which are exposing his crimes.

Everything is someone else's fault to the point where American institutions, America's promises, America's global standing, American sovereignty, and democracy itself do not matter. They don't matter to him, and they don't matter to his followers. And this is where the danger of this cultism really lies.

This is Trumpism. This is a cult. Trumpism is a cult. And it is a dangerous cult at that. What can the rest of us do about it?

Yes, Trumpism is a Cult

A cult doesn't have to be a small group of people. This one is very large, which makes it particularly dangerous.

Trumpism is unwavering devotion to a specific person; namely, Donald J. Trump. Trump supporters might consider themselves Republicans who happen to support Trump. They might consider themselves to be advocates of a certain political philosophy who happen to support Trump. But make no mistake; they are devoted to Trump, and nothing else.

When Trump picks fights with members of the Republican party, his followers always take his side over other Republicans. For heavens sake, at his rallies they shamelessly boo war hero and Republican Senator John McCain for not falling in lock step with Trump. They do this while they know perfectly well McCain is fighting for his life. It isn't just that they take Trump's side; they do so in the most shameful and anti-American ways.

As more lifetime Republicans leave the party because they don't want to be associated with Trumpism, Trump's support never wavers. When Trump attacks fellow Republicans, his support inches upward among Republicans.

Trump does not adhere to historic Republican principles. His supporters, most of whom have espoused these same principles throughout their lives, forfeit their own principles in favor of being loyal to Trump. No, Trumpism cannot rationally be explained by the "Republican who happens to support Trump" argument.

***

Why do they have unwavering loyalty to Trump? I've listened to many Trump supporters try to answer this question. None of the answers are rational within the context that they are made.

Sometimes the answer is an attack on the question itself. "He is our president, and everybody should support him instead of criticizing him". That answer would be laughable if the situation weren't quite so serious. These are the same people who, for eight years, treated President Obama as an illegitimate president – with no evidence other than conspiracy theories. Birtherism, anyone?

These are the same people who, for eight years, approved of the policy of rejecting every legislative idea that Obama supported.

Luckily, Obama was able to serve two years of his presidency with a Democratic majority in both houses of Congress. During those two years, Obama was able to pass legislation which saved the U.S. auto industry, prevented the Great Recession which he inherited from turning into a full-fledged Great Depression, and moved the economy into a quick recovery. This recovery was just as steep upwards as the free-falling recession was steep downwards.

This was accomplished with ZERO Republican votes in either House. That's right: every single Republican voted against saving the economy. They had already made an agreement to oppose every Obama policy, and they stuck to that pledge rather than help America.

Every. Single. Republican.

During those same two years, Obama was able to get his signature healthcare plan passed. Every single Republican in Congress voted against that one too, even though the plan that passed had been changed from the initial proposal to include many Republican initiatives. These initiatives were added to get some Republicans on board.

To no avail, as it turned out. Even those Republicans whose statements formed the basis for the changes voted against 20,000,000 additional Americans having access to healthcare, along with many other benefits of the Affordable Care Act.

Every. Single. Republican.

See, they had that oppose-everything-Obama-supports pledge to keep them from voting for healthcare. They even derisively named the new healthcare law "Obamacare". Republicans everywhere, not just in Congress, opposed this law even though most of them benefitted from it. After Republicans took control of Congress, they wasted time and taxpayer money by voting 60 times to "repeal Obamacare", even though they knew that their votes were politically symbolic and nothing else. They never took healthcare seriously enough to even come up with a workable alternative.

Now that they control both houses of Congress and the White House, they have made a complete mess of our healthcare system in the name of gutting Obamacare.

No, the "he is our president, and everybody should support him instead of criticizing him" argument for supporting Trump is not rational.

***

I also hear "I support Trump because he keeps his campaign promises." This simply is not true, unless the believer is talking about a specific type of promise and doesn't care about other promises.

It's true that Trump has attempted to fulfill his promises promoting hatred, bigotry, and divisiveness. Is that what the believer is talking about when he says that Trump keeps his promises?

Trump is known to contradict himself – sometimes in midsentence and sometimes by saying different things to different audiences. He also said that he would provide universal healthcare that was much better and less expensive than the ACA; he said that he would not allow Social Security, Medicaid, and Medicare benefits to be decreased; and he said that he would balance the budget. Those, and more, are promises that he has no intention of keeping. But he has kept the promise to go after the "others" in society.

***

Another reason I hear for supporting Trump is that "he speaks my language". This one is laughable, given that professional analysts have determined that Trump speaks on a 4th grade level. Does this mean that his cult members are proud of their ignorance? It's laughable. Yet given the lack of support for education in the Republican Party, it's also frightening.

The argument I hear most is "I support Trump because, despite his personal shortcomings, he will give conservatives the Supreme Court they want. We have to overlook the fact that he is a vile person, because the benefit of having him pick Supreme Court judges will be worth it in the long run."

This is the argument made by fundamentalist Christian organizations who have always railed about morality. These Bible-thumpers are the biblical equivalent of Pharisees. Their argument is not rational. They want someone who will appoint conservatives to the Supreme Court? Just about any Republican would do that. They don't need Trump.

Besides, the nominate-conservatives-to-the-Supreme-Court argument is used mostly in connection with the issue of abortion, especially by conservative Christians. Do they not know that no law can eliminate abortions completely; laws can only eliminate safe and legal abortions.

Why do these same people oppose every policy which would decrease the demand for abortions? Why do these same Bible-thumpers pass judgment on government policy, anyway? Oh, right, they don't believe in the First Amendment.

***

There is one more argument I hear for supporting Trump. This is the "We are winning because of Trump's economy" argument. The argument itself is false but it is worth mentioning because, of all the reasons to support Trump, this one has the best chance of causing supporters to leave the Trumpism cult.

In other words, if they support Trump because of the economy, they just might take away that support when the economy turns sour.

The economy has been on an upward trend since Obama's policies – the ones passed with zero votes from Republicans – ended the Great Recession in 2009. This has been the longest period of continuous economic growth in American history. The initial stimulus was followed by an economic upturn which was as fast as the downturn had been. Once this stimulus wore off, after the first few months, the economy was set on a steady – by historical standards – upward path which has continued until today.

This is the economy which Trump has taken credit for, but he inherited it. The upward trend is slightly slower under Trump than it had been under Obama, but you wouldn't know it by the rhetoric.

According to the rhetoric, the longest-ever-period-of-continuous-growth during the Obama years was merely "the slowest economic recovery in American history". Changing the word "longest" to "slowest" just to criticize Obama for something didn't change the facts. The recovery was extremely fast by historical standards and has been followed by the longest period of growth in history.

"The slowest economic recovery in American history", as Republicans kept saying, gave way to "Trump has the best economic record in American history" – and it was the same economy! The economy as of this writing is a continuation of a trend which began early in the Obama administration, only slightly slower.

No, the "we are winning because of Trump's economy" argument is not valid.

But, what will those who are making this argument going to do when the economy turns sour under Trump? It is inevitable. We are likely headed towards a recession right now, and Trump's policies are a driving force for such a downturn. These policies include a trade war and ill-conceived tax cuts for corporations and rich individuals during good economic times which are driving a mushrooming national debt.

Perhaps a Trump recession would have a silver lining. Maybe hitting millions of Trump supporters in the wallet is the one thing that could get supporters to leave the cult of Trumpism. Only time will tell.

***

The arguments given for supporting Trump do not add up logically. There must be another reason these cult members give their full support to this one man.

What kinds of people support Trump? Are they all racists?

I wouldn't say that all Trump supporters are racists, but there is a caveat. He wouldn't have had enough support to be a factor in the Republican primary of 2016 without the racist vote. He certainly wouldn't have had enough support to defeat Hillary Clinton in the general election that year (she still won the popular vote by almost 3,000,000) without the support of racists.

But racists do, indeed, comprise the base of his support. Need proof? Trump became a factor in the Republican primary through racist rants. He called Mexicans "rapists", and his poll numbers shot up. In fact, every time he made an outrageous racist comment, his poll numbers shot up. Even today, as president, his poll numbers go up whenever he says or does something with racist overtones.

You might think that a president would lose support for being racist, but Trump solidifies his support.

Does this mean that all Trump supporters are racist? Not really, but many of them certainly are. The rest of them, however, are okay enough with his racism to support him anyway. They may say that they are willing to overlook his vile remarks for some greater good, but what would be so important about supporting one man that racism is okay to overlook?

Perhaps, in a way, this kind of support is racism. I guess a willingness to overlook racism is a passive form of racism. It can be argued, then, that all Trump supporters are at least passively racist. Whether you agree with this argument or not, it requires a character flaw to support Trump knowing his racist positions and policies.

***

Does this mean that all Trump supporters are misogynists? After all, they voted for him even though it was already public knowledge that he had been credibly accused of sexual misconduct by several women. They knew that he had infamously bragged about committing sexual assault.

They knew his history with verbally abusing women for their physical appearances. They knew he had been accused of rape by one of his ex-wives. They knew that he had cheated on each of his ex-wives. They knew there is credible evidence he has cheated on his current wife.

They voted for him anyway. As more credible evidence mounts, his support only becomes more entrenched.

Does this mean that these supporters are all misogynists? I hardly think so. But misogyny is such a non-issue to them that they are willing to support Trump anyway. Such support requires a character flaw of some kind.

***

Does this mean that all Trump supporters are bullies? Bullying is a tactic that Trump uses every day. It is his go-to tactic for dealing with people when he doesn't get his way on everything. It is his go-to tactic for dealing with people who oppose him on any issue. He acts like an immature playground bully on some levels. But bullying and threatening people come so easy for him that he acts like a mafia boss on other levels.

Does this mean that all Trump supporters are bullies? Of course not. Do all Trump supporters approve of his bullying tactics? Probably not, but those attending his rallies sure do. All his supporters are at least willing to give him their unconditional devotion despite his constant bullying.

This support has damaged America. How can we teach our children to respect others when we elect a president who respects no one? A character flaw is required to support Trump while knowing that he is going to be a bully and threaten people.

***

Does this mean that all Trump supporters are anti-American, hate the Constitution, are okay with our elections being compromised by hostile foreigners, dislike democracy, disrespect our traditional military and economic allies, and approve of brutal autocrats?

I don't think very many Trump supporters would say these things. I certainly don't believe that Trump supporters are all these things. But when his followers support Trump and his attacks on investigators into these matters, they are signaling that they are okay with all these things.

This is a very dangerous part of the cult of Trumpism. Our national right to self-determination is at stake. The American way of life is at stake. The United States Constitution is at stake. Democracy itself is at stake. Why would Trump supporters be willing to risk all of this and continue to support him? What could be more important to them?

Even if they want to believe that Trump is innocent of any charges, why would they choose to risk everything by not allowing a full investigation?

Trump supporters have access to the same information that scares the rest of us to death. Why do they double-down on their support every time some new details emerge? Perhaps they aren't paying attention to the facts. Perhaps they believe Trump every time he Tweets "Fake News!"

Are all Trump supporters serial liars? Trump sure is. When his supporters have access to the truth, but choose to believe untruths instead, they most certainly show disregard for the truth. This includes every Trump supporter. If they respected the truth, they wouldn't be Trump supporters. What kind of example does this set for our children?

Willful ignorance is not a virtue when so much is on the line. Willful ignorance, in fact, is a character flaw. But cult members are conditioned to treat negative information as an unfair attack on the cult leader. Trumpism is a cult.

***

Trump supporters must be willing to support him despite his…

Racist rants and racist policies

Horrible treatment of women

Repetitive bullying tactics

Disregard for the U.S. Constitution

Animosity towards vital American institutions

Animosity towards long-standing American military allies

Admiration for Putin and other murderous dictators

Picking fights and trade wars with key trading partners

Willingness to renege on America's promises

Attacks on democratic processes

Autocratic tendencies

Total disregard for the truth

***

There simply are no rational reasons for saying all of this is somehow worth it. It takes serious character flaws to support Trump when he carries this much baggage.

You don't have to be a Trump supporter to have character flaws. But you do have to have character flaws to be a Trump supporter. It is a necessary condition.

Only cult members protecting their messiah would be willing to put the United States through all of this.

Putin and Russia are the Beneficiaries

Trump keeps saying that he has been tougher on Russia than his predecessors were. While this statement is false, his intended audience is his cult. He knows they will believe what he tells them.

In truth, an American president couldn't do more to help Putin and Russia if he tried. The big question is, has Trump been trying to help Russia? Time and Robert Mueller will tell. The Special Counsel has more information than we do.

Consider the following publicly-known information:

Following secret meetings between Trump campaign leaders and Russians, the Trump campaign insisted that the 2016 Republican National Convention platform be changed in only one way: to soften language critical of Russia.

Trump transition officials secretly met with Russians and illegally promised to undo sanctions imposed by the Obama administration. After the inauguration, Trump attempted to follow up on this promise.

When Congress passed new sanctions against Russia, Trump refused to enforce them.

Trump's actions have weakened NATO and other western arrangements. This is like a dream come true for Putin.

Trump is deliberately undermining the integrity of United States intelligence agencies; just what Russia wants to happen.

Trump is blowing up the G7, in part by insisting that Russia should be allowed back in.

How Can We Save America from this Madness?

Donald Trump is one man. Yes, he has done tremendous damage to America. But America and her institutions are strong. Many Americans are speaking out against Trump and the damage he has caused. If the people demand it, we will be okay.

Trump and the damage he has created can be stopped. It will take years to undo this damage. It might take decades to undo some of it. This is some serious damage, after all. How long it takes depends on what the people demand, and the willingness of Congress to do what is necessary.

All members of Congress have taken an oath of office. When the full story behind these scandals is made public, will we have a Congress willing to abide by this oath?

We can stop Trump. The question is whether we can stop Trumpism. Trumpism is more than one man. Trumpism is a cult comprised of millions of Americans who are willing to defy America's institutions when they conflict with the notion that Trump is the "true leader". What will these people do when Trump is held accountable? Will they go to war against America?

This is a serious question. Trump's supporters knew what kind of person he was before they voted for him. They have lived through the damage he is doing to America. Yet his support has not waned. Instead, his supporters dig in deeper with every new revelation. They dig in deeper every time he says and does the most outrageous things. They have taken his side in every fight he has waged against American institutions.

Trump's supporters have shown a willingness to risk America's future, and democracy itself, rather than leave the cult of Trumpism. He has been conditioning them to not accept the findings of the intelligence community. What happens if they don't accept the truth when it is all revealed? What happens to America?

We don't know what they will do. We do know that they number in the millions, and we are going to have to live with them after Trump is gone. How is that possible?

We must find a way, that's all.

At the end of the American Civil War, President Lincoln did not wish to punish those who fought for the Confederacy against the United States. He chose to welcome them back with full American citizenship. He was willing to forgive everything. The goal of the war, from his perspective, had always been reunification. These were very generous terms from the victorious side. Acceptance of them was up to those from the South. From a historical perspective, the results have been mixed at best. No one knows how it would have turned out if Lincoln had been alive to lead the effort during his second term in office.

This time is a little different. What happens if the Trump cult takes up arms against America and refuses to accept the truth? We simply don't know. Thinking about it is frightening indeed.

We aren't there yet. Hopefully, we will never have to deal with such an uprising. Why should we even think that such a thing would be possible? The answer is that with the combination of unwavering cultish loyalty and being conditioned to not trust the intelligence community and others, they seem capable of just about anything. Maybe there will be trouble, maybe they will accept the outcome. We simply do not know.

But what should we do in the meantime?

In normal times, we could remain civil about political differences. We could speak up and state our case. Democracy isn't a spectator sport, and sometimes it is ugly. Sometimes, progress is very slow, nearly undetectable. But if we are on the right side, eventually the truth will come out.

These are not normal times, however. We are dealing with a cult willing to give up everything to protect their leader. What happens if Trump must be removed because of his misdeeds, and the cult won't accept such an outcome? What happens if they do, indeed, take up arms against America, and we could have done something to stop it?

What can we do? Should we continue to state the case for sanity, knowing that they won't listen? Should we continue to allow the situation to get worse and worse, and sit back and wait? The answers are not easy. These are not normal times. It's not like we can hold an intervention for millions of cult members. Or can we?

Just like the Civil War often pitted brother against brother, this cult of Trumpism has torn families apart. Which is the best course of action: politely agree to disagree, or impolitely walk away from these cult members, destroying your family and long-term relationships? Which is the best way to move America away from this nightmarish situation?

I don't know the answers to those questions. I do know that to undo the damage and prevent it from happening again, a lot of things must change. This means Congress must take back the constitutional duties it has abdicated. It means, in fact, a lot of legislative action. This will take a long time. I don't want to be accused of advocating for one-party rule, but to fix this properly, we will need Democrats in Congress leading the way. Republicans in Congress today have proven themselves to be part of the problem.

This is my 6th published book